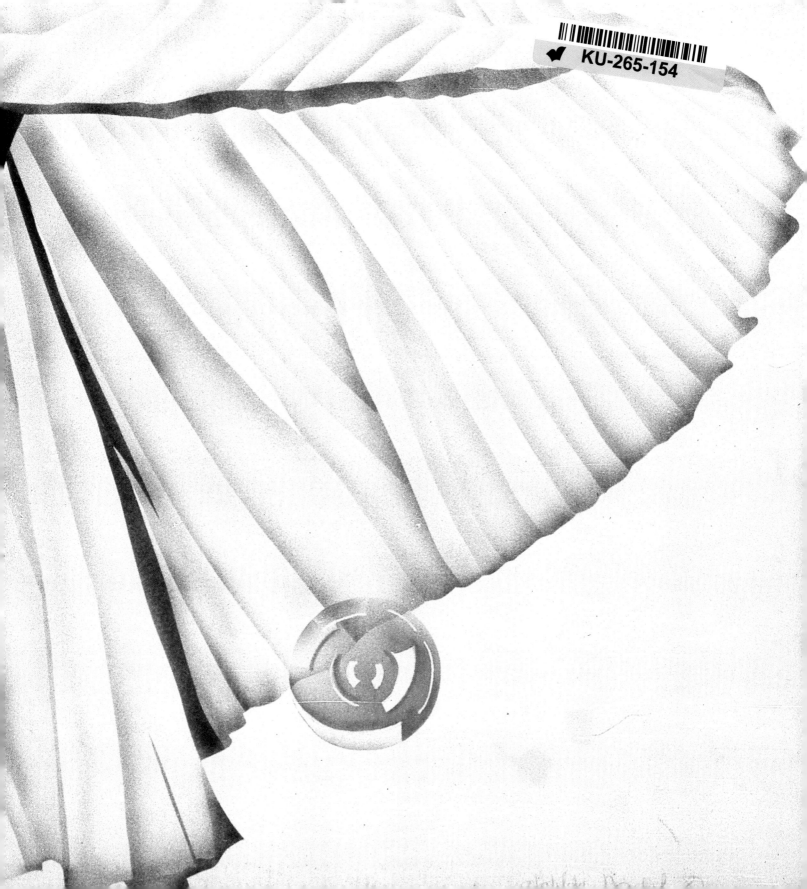

MARILYN IN ART

Leon Garcia/Garcia Designs Ltd

MARILYN
IN ART

COMPILED BY
ROGER G TAYLOR

ELM TREE BOOKS LONDON

This book is dedicated to my family,
with love.

Design by Craig Dodd

First published in Great Britain 1984
by Elm Tree Books/Hamish Hamilton Ltd
Garden House 57-59 Long Acre London WC2E 9JZ

Introduction and collection copyright © 1984 by Roger Taylor

British Library Cataloguing in Publication Data

Taylor, Roger G.
   Marilyn in art.
   1. Monroe, Marilyn—Portraits, etc.
   2. Art, Modern—20th century
   I. Title
   760'.04424   N7639.M6

   ISBN 0-241-11326-1

Printed in Italy by New Interlitho, Milan

FOREWORD

Who will argue with us that the image of Marilyn Monroe, perhaps the most celebrated woman in the world at the time of her death in 1962, remains one of the most potent and reverberative of our times. She was once described as 'the sweet angel of sex', an incisive epithet that captures the contradictions and paradoxes that make up her story – those of waiflike innocence yet glittering eroticism, of worldliness yet profound vulnerability. By any standards her film career was brief, yet from a few thousand feet of celluloid has crystallised a pre-eminent media persona, so highly individualistic that she was called 'the only blonde in the world.' Her films are now played endlessly in video, reproductions of Warhol's zomboid portraits of her hang in a million homes, and friends and lovers throughout the world send subdued sexual messages to each other on greetings cards bearing her likeness. The impermanent image of Monroe flickering at speed upon a cinema screen, or captured in the posed perfection of the studio portrait, possesses a remarkable allure; it is an appeal that eventually could hardly fail to attract many artists, so much so that their works depicting her have multiplied inexorably, and they are brought together here for the first time.

The paintings and drawings that make up this book come from many sources. Though a handful of them are to be found displayed in the elegant and ordered world of the major art galleries, the greater number are products of the popular presses – books, magazines, film journals, and the exuberant billboard art of the Californian graphics studios, all offer up their version of Marilyn Monroe, raising her to that elite body of the media legends. In their turn, an elite group of the art world's own celebrities have turned to Monroe for their inspiration. Andy Warhol's standardised, fixated Marilyn has become perhaps the most famous portrait of her, an exemplar of mass imagery at its most pervasive; yet this contemporary icon offers but one perspective of her, and its automatic and repetitive style is exactly counterpoised by Willem deKooning's frenzied and distorted presentation of Monroe. The art historian Peter Selz identifies the underlying malaise:

'Throughout the ages, artists have made symbols of female goddesses and cult images. DeKooning has painted them as masochistic, shamelessly erotic women whose distortion expresses great suffering.'

That deKooning and others of his distinction have chosen Marilyn Monroe as subject, and have reiterated the symbolic nature of her sexual qualities, is perhaps the most persuasive evidence that we have of the extent to which she has come to epitomise popular notions of the beautiful and the erotic. Yet Monroe belonged originally not to canvas or paper, but to film; it was film that brought her to the public's consciousness, and film that emphasised and re-emphasised her presence. When the studio was not the source, then the press photographer was ready to capture the telling picture that showed Marilyn as all thought she must be – bold, flamboyant, glamorous. It is not surprising, therefore, that so many of the paintings and drawings made of her have traded on the dazzling vitality of those photographs. If not simple transformations into paint of well-known camera studies, then they are composites drawn from the photographic cornucopia that her public and private lives engendered. Eerie photo-realistic paintings included here trick the eye with paint just as do chemicals upon celluloid film. At the other extreme, stylised, expressionistic, or even abstract representations of her still depend upon the instantly recognisable attributes – the sensual mouth half open, the dreaming sultry eyes, the heavy breasts less fully known to the world than those of the newer love goddesses – each the perfect cue to be given to the viewer, that here is something that is familiar and mostly Monroe. Artistic licence has been exercised in full, as inevitably it must be with so rich a visual subject, but there is little here that does not connect at some point with the original model in all its excellence.

In the provocative and disquieting quality of some of the pictures in this collection, a mirror is perhaps held up to her brief and sometimes troubled life. The now well-known story of relentless ambition countered by desperate insecurity, of a glamorous outward aura surrounding a fragile personality, is also that of a woman possessed of a simple but irresistible personal magnetism, illustrated vividly by an anecdote recounted by Amy Greene, wife of Marilyn's closest friend, Milton Greene. Sinatra is appearing at the Copacabana in New York, and Amy Greene suggests that it would be exciting to see him; immediately Marilyn orders her to dress, and two hours later they are at the doors of the Copacabana. Marilyn is in a white dress and white furs:

'We had no reservations, of course, not even a phone call for warning, and Marilyn smiled at the dragon who was standing at the door and he fell back, and we just moved forward through Mafia bouncer after Mafia bouncer until we got to the room where Sinatra was singing, and of course there wasn't a seat available or even an *aisle* for that matter, and Marilyn just stood at the rear of the room not moving and one by one the customers turned to look at her and the show slowly stopped and Sinatra finally saw her, and said, "Waiter, bring a table here," and we were conducted, we were virtually *carried* through these nightclub *gargoyles* at their tables with their wives and their mistresses after they'd schemed and begged for reservations and of course we were put directly under Sinatra and his microphone, there could not have been a space closer to him, God *knows* what they did to the people they pushed back, and then Milton, Marilyn, and I were sung to by Sinatra, he sang the entire set to us alone, and in the middle, Marilyn kicked me in the foot and said, "You like the table?" "Bitch!" I whispered back.'

Time and again artists have dissected, analysed, and re-assembled the image of this remarkable woman in their work, and in so doing have affirmed her posthumous stature as symbol and the mythical status acquired by simple virtue of her death. *Eros* and *thanatos*: those whom the media love often die young. Warhol's oft-repeated dictum that 'in the future everyone will be famous for fifteen minutes' is meant to remind us that fame is most often fleeting, a transient diversion from the ordinary and the predictable. But not so for Marilyn Monroe. Hers is a unique and universal fame that two decades after her death shows no signs of diminishing.

Acknowledgements

The author would like to thank Peter J. Taylor for all his help,
support and guidance with this project.
Very special thanks to:

Rhona F. Levene   Ken Rogers   Stephanie Lipton
Garey Gadson   Paul Huf
Mize   Charlie   Valerie Boyd
Ed Mason, Chelsea Antique Market, Shop 5, 253 Kings Road, London SW3
Roy's Restaurant, 206 Fulham Road, London SW10

And to all the artists for their cooperation
and their contributions to this project.

The lyrics of *Candle in the Wind*, composed by Elton John and Bernie Taupin
© 1973 Dick James Music Ltd, London

'Never a week passes when I don't wish she was still around.'

Billy Wilder

'She owned nothing in her life, least of all herself. As servant, the public adored her to the point of neglect. They built a pedestal for their mistress so high that they could not reach her, nor she them. The result was that she died of affection by adoration. To summarise simply: she did a lot for us, and we did nothing for her'.

Paul Mayersberg

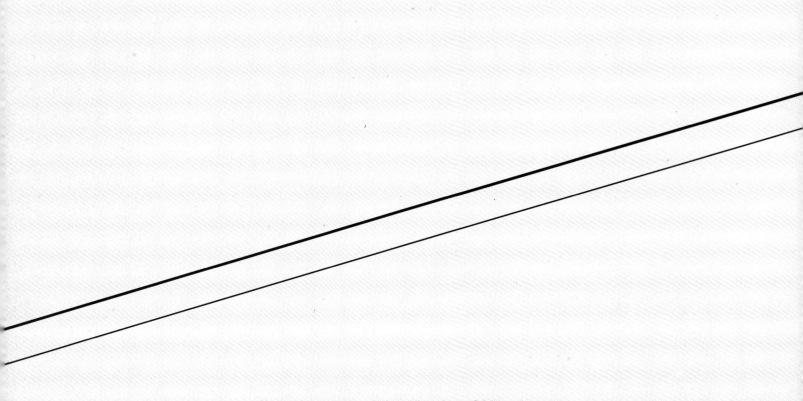

'She has an innocence which is so extraordinary, whatever she plays, however brazen a hussy, it always comes out as an innocent girl. I remember Sir Laurence saying one day during the filming: "Look at that face – she could be five years old."'

Dame Sybil Thorndike

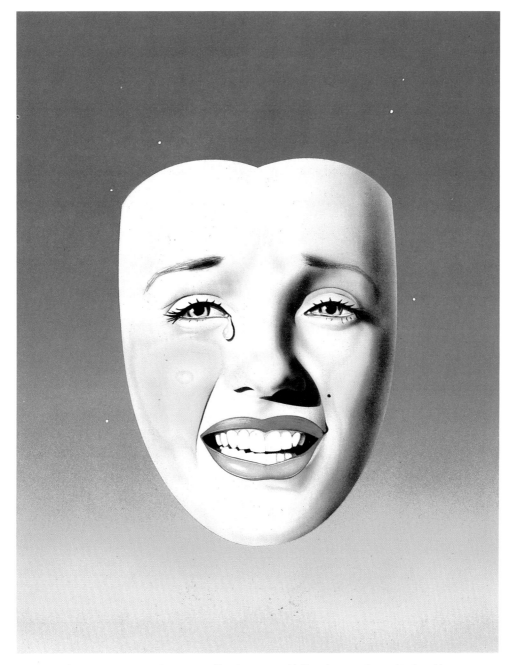

'On the surface, she was still a happy girl. But those who criticised her never saw her as I did, crying like a baby because she often felt herself so inadequate. Sometimes she suffered terrific depressions, and would even talk about death.'

Bill Travilla

michel faure

'I suppose all the sob sisters in the world will now start to go to work. In a way we're all guilty. We built her up to the skies, we loved her, but we left her lonely and afraid when she needed us most.'

Hedda Hopper

'Our feelings about Marilyn Monroe have been so coloured by her death and not simply, as the uncharitable would have us think, because she is no longer an irritation or a threat, but because her suicide, as suicides do, casts a retrospective light on her life. "Her ending" gives her a beginning and middle, turns her into a work of art with a message and a meaning.'

Molly Haskell

'Still she hangs like a bat in the heads of the men who met her, and none of us will ever forget her.'

Sammy Davis Jr

'I think she's something different to each man, blending somehow the
things he seems to require most.'

Clark Gable

'In Hollywood a girl's virtue is much less important than her hair-do. You're judged by how you look, not by what you are. Hollywood's a place where they'll pay you a thousand dollars for a kiss, and fifty cents for your soul. I know, because I turned down the first offer often enough and held out for the fifty cents.'

Marilyn Monroe

'When you're a failure in Hollywood, that's like starving to death outside a banquet hall with smells of filet mignon driving you crazy.'

Marilyn Monroe

'It wasn't Hollywood that destroyed her – she was a victim of her friends.'

Joe DiMaggio

M. DOLACK · 82

'In her own lifetime she created a myth of what a poor girl from a deprived background could attain. For the entire world she became a symbol of the eternal feminine — I hope that her death will stir sympathy and understanding for a sensitive artist and woman who brought joy and pleasure to the world.'

Lee Strasberg

'When you look at Marilyn on the screen, you don't want anything bad to happen to her. You really care that she should be all right … happy.'

Natalie Wood

'Marilyn is a simple girl, without any guile. I once thought she was sophisticated like some of the other ladies I have known. Had Marilyn been sophisticated, none of this ever would have happened.'

Yves Montand

'It can be no news to anyone to say that she was difficult to work with. Her work frightened her, and although she had undoubted talent, I think she had a subconscious resistance to the exercise of being an actress. But she was intrigued by its mystique and happy as a child when being photographed; she managed all the business of stardom with uncanny, clever, apparent ease.'

Laurence Olivier

michel Faure

'Marilyn was history's most phenomenal love-goddess. Why? Most people think the reason was self-evident, especially when she wore a snug evening gown. But there are other girls who have outstanding figures. Paradoxically, Marilyn's very weakness was her great strength. Her inferiority complex, her pathetic, almost childlike need for security are the very things that made her irresistible.'

Philippe Halsman

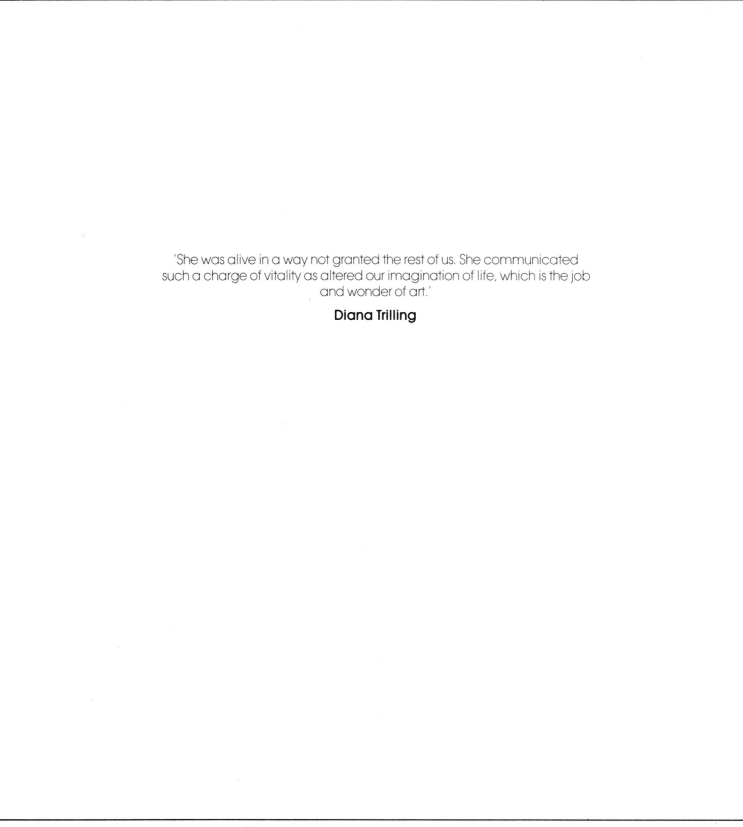

'She was alive in a way not granted the rest of us. She communicated
such a charge of vitality as altered our imagination of life, which is the job
and wonder of art.'

Diana Trilling

michel faure

'A perfect body like Marilyn's looks beautiful nude, and beauty is never vulgar. Her animal magnetism, though sometimes flamboyant, always had an appealing, childlike quality which seemed to be poking fun at the very quality she symbolised.'

Agnes Flanagan
Marilyn's hair stylist

'At various times her immense appeal was attributed to her breathless voice, her incandescence, her ash blonde hair, her moist-lipped mouth, her dreamy blue eyes, and that tremulous gait. It was more elusive than that – and more earthy. Marilyn's need to be desired was so great that she could make love to a camera. Because of this, her lust aroused lust in audiences, sometimes even among women. There was nothing subtle about it. She was no tease. She was prepared, and even eager, to give what she offered.'

William Manchester

Pepe Gonzalez

"El sexo es una parte de la naturaleza. Yo estoy del lado de la naturaleza"

MM

¡Socorro, socorro, Socorro. Siento la vida acercarse... Cuando todo lo que deseo es morir.

(Poema de MM)

Pepe Gonzalez

me gusta estar
rdaderamente vestida
completamente desnuda
o me gustan las
medias tintas"
    M M

'You can take every possible identifiable ingredient that she had and put them together and mix them, and add in the date and the number you first thought of, and at the end of it, all you've got is a blonde, a small girl with a sweet face and a terrifically voluptuous body, but you still haven't got Marilyn Monroe.'

Barry Norman

'A great force of nature, she was becoming a victim of the propaganda machine, of her own struggle to build herself up. About her swirled a hurricane, and she was its eye. She longed for privacy, but she had murdered privacy, as Macbeth had murdered sleep. Her time was not hers. And her personality was not hers.'

Maurice Zolotow
biographer

Pepe Gonzalez

Pepe Gonzalez

'Marilyn made me lose all sympathy for actresses. In most of her takes she was either fluffing lines or freezing. She didn't bother to learn lines. I don't think she could act her way out of a paper script. She has no charm, delicacy or taste. She's just an arrogant little tail switcher who's learned how to throw sex in your face.'

Nunally Johnson
writer/producer

'Not having seen Miss Monroe before, I know now what that's all about, and I've no dissenting opinions to offer. She disproves more than adequately the efficacy of the old stage rule about not turning one's back to the audience.'

Paul V. Beckley
critic

'There's a broad with her future behind her.'

Constance Bennett

'Marilyn's attitude toward her make-up and costumes was courageous.
Incredible really. Here you have a well-established star. She was willing to
risk her position with a make-up many stars would have considered ugly.
She wasn't afraid. She believed she was right in her analysis of the
character, and she had the courage to commit herself to it completely.'

Joshua Logan

Daniel Tarantola

'I think she's rather vulgar. Not in language. I never heard her swear in my presence, although I'm sure she knows how, but there's vulgarity in the way she dresses and behaves off camera. No one around her dares criticise her in any way. She's a queen surrounded by her courtiers.'

Angela Allen
John Huston's script supervisor

Daniel Tarantola

'There's been an awful lot of crap written about Marilyn Monroe, and there may be an exact psychiatric term for what was wrong with her. I don't know – but truth to tell I think she was quite mad. The mother was mad, and poor Marilyn was mad. I know people who say "Hollywood broke her heart" and all that, but I don't believe it. She was very observant and tough-minded and appealing, but she had this bad judgement about things. She adored and trusted the wrong people. She was very courageous – you know that book *Twelve Against the Gods*? Marilyn was like that. She had to challenge the Gods at every turn, and eventually she lost.'

George Cukor

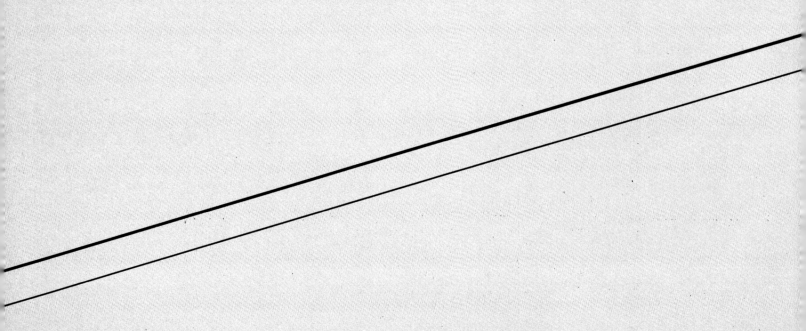

'Marilyn was an incredible person to act with ... the most marvellous I ever worked with, and I have been working for 29 years. But she went over the fringe. Playing a scene with her, it was like an escalator. You'd do something and she'd catch it and it would go like that, just right up.'

Montgomery Clift

'I'd have been upset, you know, if there were 20,000 people watching my wife's skirt blow over her head.'

Billy Wilder

'She stood for life. She radiated life. In her smile hope was always present.
She glorified in life, and her death did not mar this final image. She had
become a legend in her own time, and in her death took her place
among the myths of our century.'

John Kobal

'Moscow is the only city where, if Marilyn Monroe walked down the street with nothing on but a pair of shoes, people would stare at her feet first.'

John Gunther
Inside Russia Today, 1962

'I think Marilyn was as mad as a hatter.'

Tony Curtis

David Reeson

I KNEW AN OLD LADY WHO SWALLOWED A CONCORDE

Once, across the years, she sent Norman Rosten a postcard with a colour photograph of an American Airlines jet in the sky, and on the back in the space for the messgage, she put down, `Guess where I am, Love Marilyn'.

ONE IN EVERY CROWD

'She had such magnetism that if fifteen men were in a room with her,
each man would be convinced he was the one she'd be waiting for after
the others left.'

Roy Craft

'Girls ask me all the time how they can be like Marilyn Monroe. And I tell them, if they showed one tenth of the hard work and gumption that that girl had, they'd be on their way. But there will never be another like her.'

'The graduate I am most proud of is Marilyn Monroe. Not only because she is the most successful and well known of my students, but because she started with the least. She was cute-looking, but she knew nothing about carriage, posture, walking, sitting or posing.'

Emmeline Snively
founder of Blue Books Model School

Daniel Tarantola

'I got a cold chill. This girl had something I hadn't seen since silent pictures. She had a kind of fantastic beauty like Gloria Swanson, and she radiated sex like Jean Harlow. She didn't need a soundtrack to tell her story.'

Leon Shamroy

'She had flesh which photographs like flesh. You feel you can reach out and touch it.'

Billy Wilder

Tom T. Tomita/Windermere Press Inc

'So we think of Marilyn who was every man's love affair with America. Marilyn Monroe who was blonde and beautiful and had a sweet little rinky-dink of a voice and all the cleanliness of all the clean American backyards. She was our angel, the sweet angel of sex, and the sugar of sex came up from her like a resonance of sound in the clearest grain of a violin. Across five continents the men who knew the most about love would covet her, and the classical pimples of the adolescent working his first gas pump would also pump for her, since Marilyn was deliverance, a very Stradivarius of sex, so gorgeous, forgiving, humorous, compliant and tender that even the most mediocre musician would relax his lack of art in the dissolving magic of her violin.'

Norman Mailer

'I have never met anyone as utterly mean as Marilyn Monroe. Nor as
utterly fabulous on the screen, and that includes Garbo.'

Billy Wilder

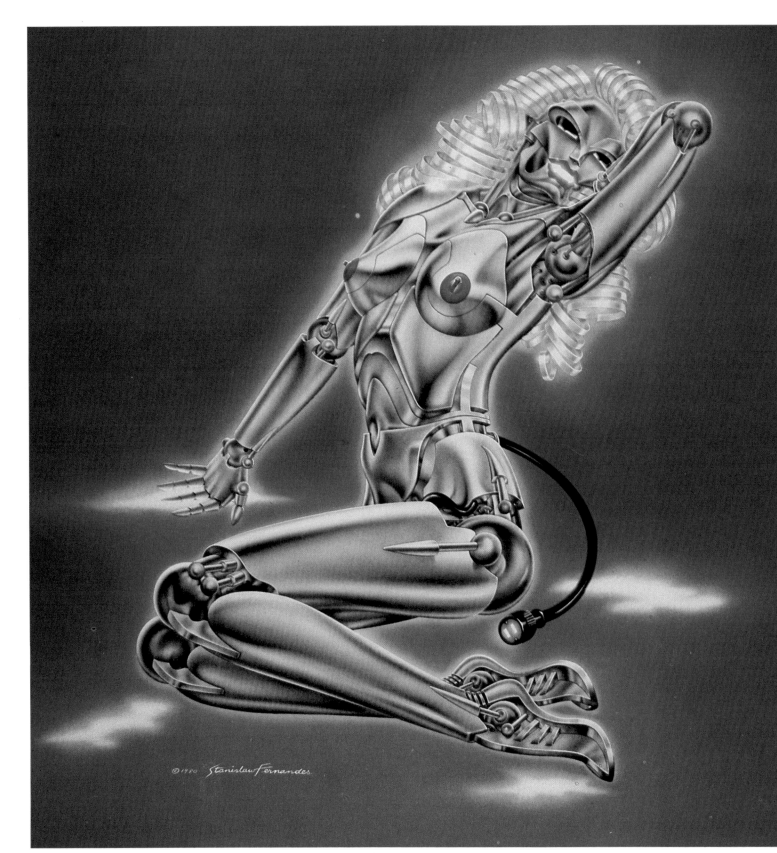

©1980 Stanislaw Fernandes

'Marilyn actively wanted humanisation and emotionally she fought against becoming a symbol or an object. To be sexually attractive was one thing, but to become a sexual fetish was another. Marilyn Monroe became a pair of lips, a walk, a set of numbers 38-24-36.'

Paul Mayersberg

'She's basically a good girl, but what's happened to her is enough to drive almost anybody slightly daffy, even someone whose background has armoured her with poise and calmness. But you take a girl like Marilyn, who's never had a chance to learn, who's never had a chance to live, and you suddenly confront her with a Frankenstein's monster of herself built of fame and publicity and notoriety, and naturally she's a little mixed up and made giddy by it all.'

Billy Wilder

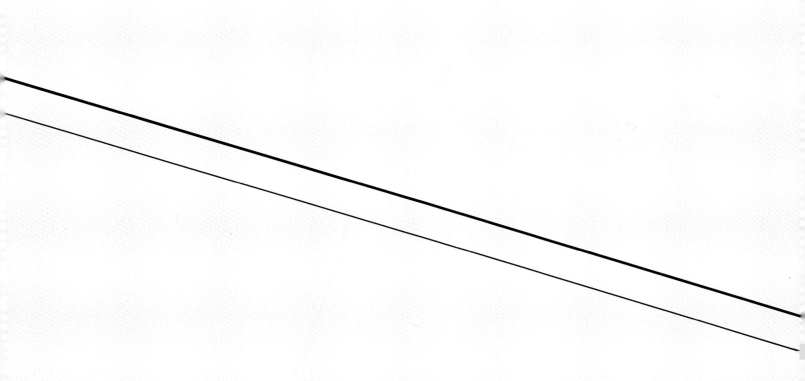

Bonbon Marilyn by Mori Bund, courtesy of Paul Huf

'She's American, and it's very clear that she is … she's very good that way
… one has to be very local to be universal.'

Henry Cartier-Bresson

'When we think of the American way of life, we think of bubble-gum,
coca-cola, and Marilyn Monroe.'

Nadya
Russian Journal

Greetings from

'None but Marilyn Monroe could suggest such a purity of sexual delight. The boldness with which she could parade herself and yet never be gross, her sexual flamboyance and bravado which yet breathed an air of mystery and even reticence, her voice which carried such ripe overtones of erotic excitement and yet was the voice of a shy child – these complications were integral to her gift. And they described a young woman trapped in some never-never land of unawareness.'

Diana Trilling

Roger G. Taylor

'There's something extremely alert and vivid in her, an intelligence. It's her personality, it's a glance, it's something very tenuous, very vivid that disappears quickly, that appears again.'

Henri Cartier-Bresson

Roger G. Taylor

'Marilyn was forced to submerge herself in her own myth. She had fantasies as a child like we all do, but those fantasies became realities. She had all this personality and she had to play that role. I saw her in her bathrobe, running around in slippers, and she had a little voice and a big voice. The public only knew the little voice. I knew the big voice. She not only married the intellectual Arthur Miller, she married Joe DiMaggio. She was obviously searching for something but she couldn't find it.'

Larry Schiller
photographer

'I don't mind being burdened with being glamorous and sexual. But what goes with it can be a burden. I feel that beauty and femininity are ageless and can't be contrived, and glamour – although manufacturers won't like this – cannot be manufactured. Not a real glamour, it's based on femininity. I think that sexuality is only attractive when it's natural and spontaneous. We are all born sexual creatures, thank God, but it's a pity so many people despise and crush this natural gift. Art, real art, comes from it – everything.'

Marilyn Monroe

'People had a habit of looking at me as if I were some kind of mirror instead of a person. They didn't see me, they saw their own lewd thoughts, then they white-masked themselves by calling me the lewd one.'

Marilyn Monroe

'Unique is an overworked word, but in her case it applies. There will never be another like her, and Lord knows there have been plenty of imitations.'

Billy Wilder

'She understood photography, and she also understood what makes a great photograph – not the technique, but the content … she was more comfortable in front of the camera than away from it … she was completely creative … she was very, very involved with the meaning of what she was doing, in an effort to make it more, to get the most out of it.'

Richard Avedon

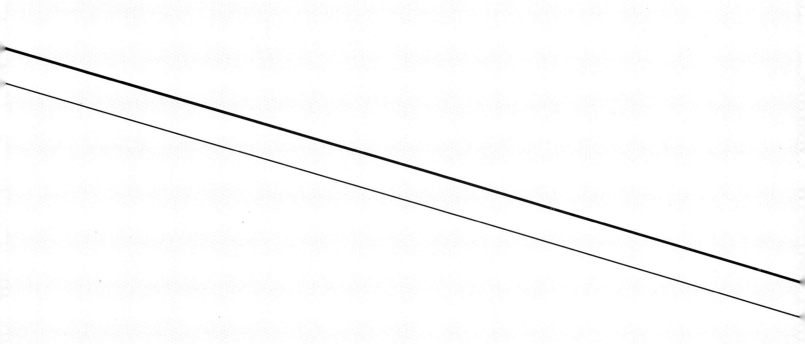

Ben Verkaaik

'The great success of Monroe, I think, was that she did not infuriate the female. If I told my wife after I worked with Monroe, "My God, I'm crazy about her," she says she would understand it. But if I told her, "By God, do I wish I could spend a night with Farrah Fawcett-Majors," she would hit me in the mouth.'

Billy Wilder

'She was the bastard daughter of a paranoid schizophrenic … a girl with a desperate, insatiable yearning to be wanted … her first husband taught her sexual ecstasy on a Murphy bed. She gloried in it and would pursue it for the rest of her life, but it wasn't enough; she craved the adoration of millions.'

William Manchester
The Glory and the Dream

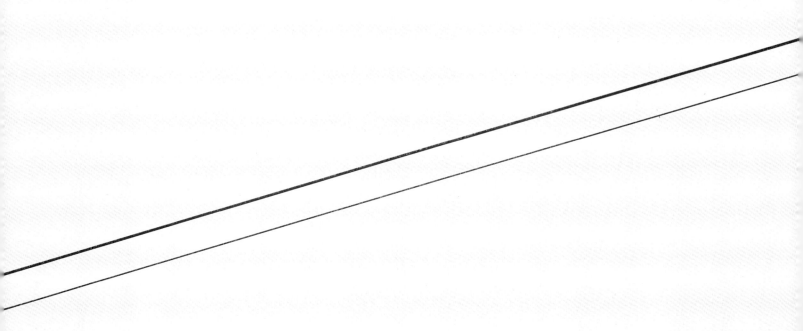

David Ward/The Paper House Ltd

PLAYBILL

JOHN GOLDEN THEATRE

KENNEDY'S CHILDREN

'I can now retire from politics after having had "Happy Birthday" sung to
me by such a sweet, wholesome girl as Marilyn Monroe.'

Jack Kennedy

Marilyn!

THE MUSICAL

'I didn't discover Marilyn Monroe. Marilyn discovered herself through the eyes of her adoring public.'

Darryl Zanuck

Designed and printed by Dewynters Ltd

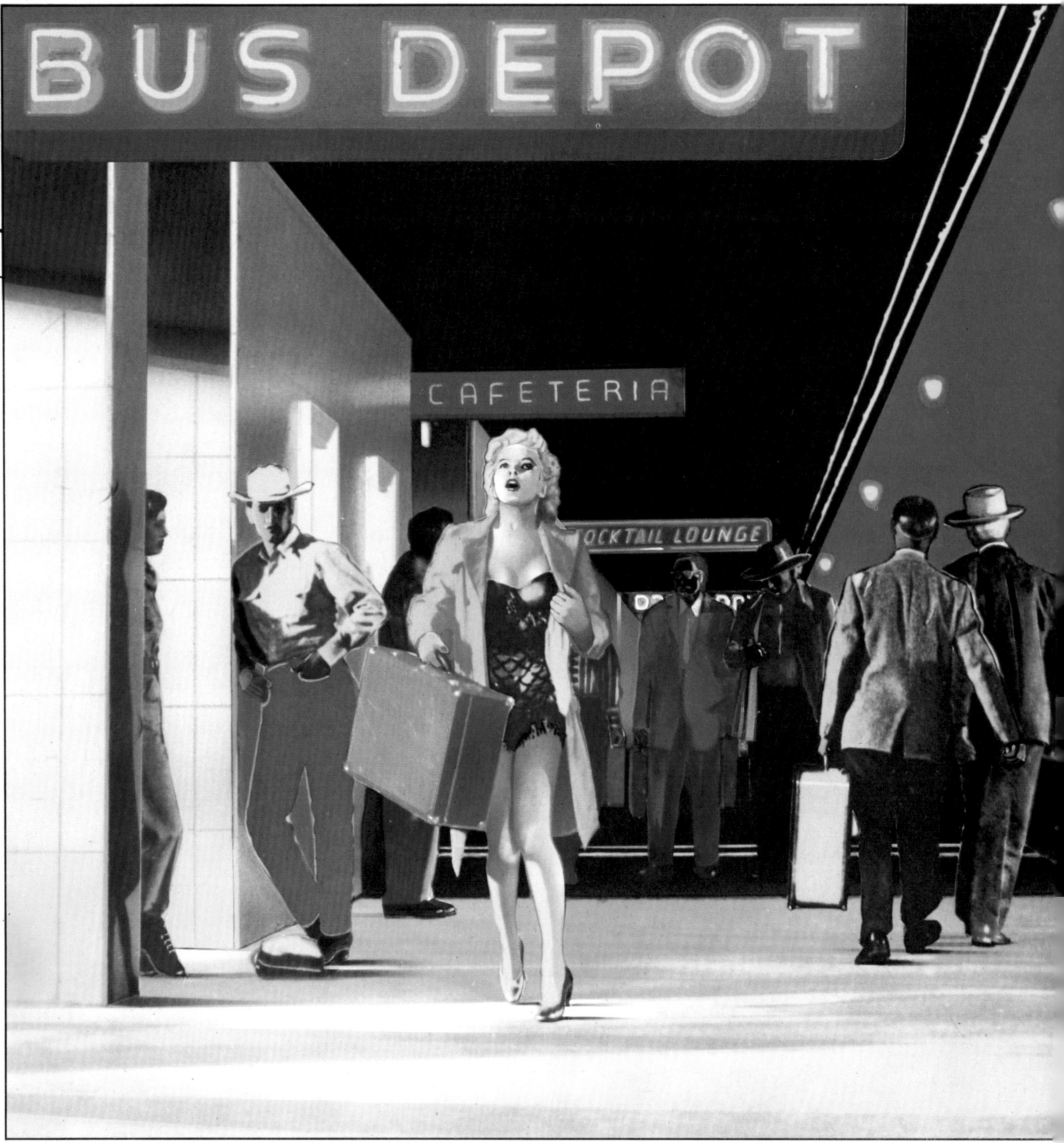
BUS DEPOT
CAFETERIA
OCKTAIL LOUNGE

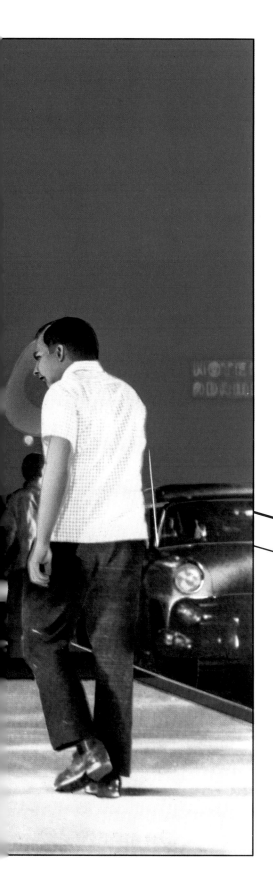

'She was a very peculiar mixture of shyness and uncertainty and – I wouldn't say "star allure" – but she knew exactly her impact on men.'

Fritz Lang

Marilyn Monroe as Chérie. Jan Hunt/Verkerke copyright and licensing gmbh

'She had this absolute, unerring touch with comedy. In real life she didn't seem funny, but she had this touch. She acted as if she didn't quite understand why it was funny, which is what made it so funny. She could also do low comedy – pratfalls and things like that – but I think her friends told her it wasn't worthy of her. As a director, I really had very little influence on her. All I could do was make a climate that was agreeable to her. Every day was an agony for her, just to get there. It wasn't just wilfulness, it was … like the comedy, something she didn't seem to understand.'

George Cukor

Goodbye Norma Jean
Though I never knew you at all
You had the grace to hold yourself
While those around you crawled
Goodbye Norma Jean
From the young man in the 22nd row
Who sees you as something more than sexual
More than just our Marilyn Monroe.

Elton John

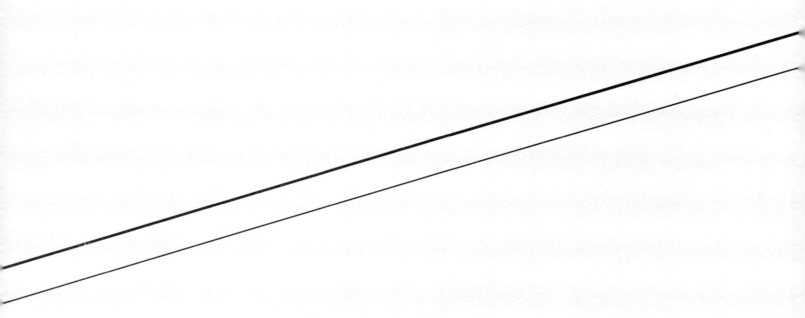

David Oxtoby/Miki Slingsby Fine Art Photography

Average female box-office unit drawn in relative proportion

Marilyn Monroe

How to Marry a Millionaire   1953

Marilyn Monroe   Joseph Cotten   Jean Peters

Niagara   1953

'I thought, surely she won't come over, she's so small scale, but when I saw her on the screen, my goodness how it came over.'

Dame Sybil Thorndike

'It is a disease of our profession that we believe a woman with physical appeal has no talent. Marilyn is as near a genius as any actress I ever knew. She is an artist beyond artistry. She is the most completely realised and authentic film actress since Garbo. She has that same unfathomable mysteriousness. She is pure cinema.'

Joshua Logan

'She loved it, when I photographed her in the nude. She loved it.
Everything was gone, she'd take her clothes off. You know, she wasn't that
busty and she had a little heavy hips. And there were some varicose veins
in there. And she had freckles all over. She was just like the girl next door.

Larry Schiller

'I look at them now [his series of paintings of women made in the early 1950s] and they seem vociferous and ferocious. I think it had to do with the idea of the idol, the oracle, and above all the hilariousness of it.'

Willem deKooning

'As I was writing this, news came of the presumed suicide of Marilyn Monroe, who always seemed among the more appealing of the tinsel goddesses of Hollywood. Her passing was important, everyone agreed, because she had become a "symbol". Symbol or no, her real virtue was an unpretentiousness that even the most artful publicity flacks could not efface: she hated being regarded as a "thing" and was candid about her opinions, which the priggish would regard as less than respectable. Yet the nature of her death, ironically, will turn her more than ever into a "thing", a cult figure in the necrophiliac rites that already surround another symbol – James Dean.'

Malcom Muggeridge

'... Sex plays a tremendously important part in every person's life. People are interested in it, intrigued with it. But they don't like to see it flaunted in their faces ... the publicity has gone too far. She is making the mistake of believing her publicity. She should be told that the public likes provocative feminine personalities, but it also likes to know that underneath it all, the actresses are ladies.'

Joan Crawford

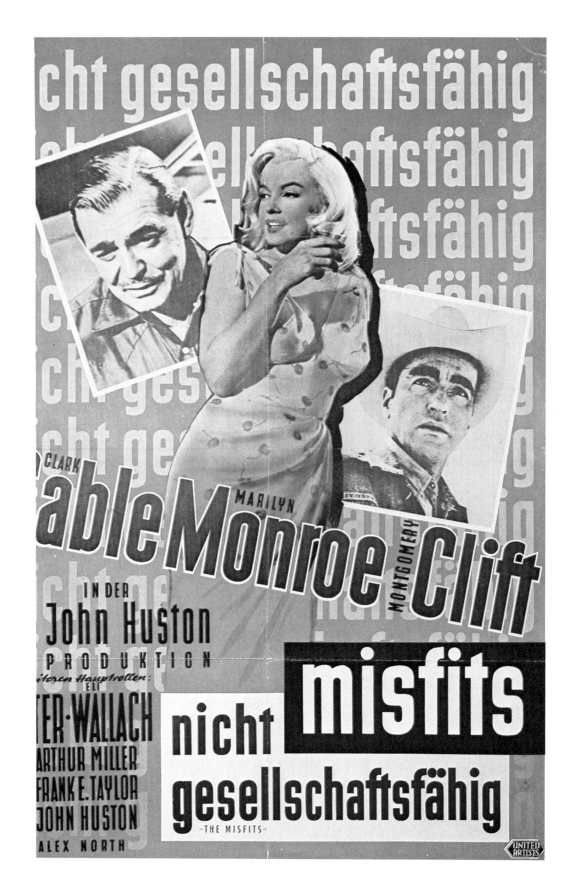

'Gable's old masculine ethics no longer worked against a sex goddess like Marilyn Monroe. This was a woman he could not clout on the jaw – maybe earlier in her career, he might have, but not now – for in the film she is hardly corporeal. Monroe's Roslyn is less of a sex symbol than a nature symbol – a species that offers few hand-holds for a determined man of action. She exists in the moonlight she dances in, in the leaves of grass Gable walks on, in the suffering wild life that he, in his Hemingway outlook, has thought to be only good for pot shots. When brute force meets the life force, it is the former that has to yield. The aspects of a woman which make her lovable in the abstract often turn disturbingly into neurotic reflexes that are unlivable with in practical life. Arthur Miller's screenplay, which has been taken as a celebration of his wife, sometimes has more the flavour of an attempt to exorcise her – and Gable was the body on whom all her ethereal qualities were projected, bewitchingly at first, then perplexingly, frustratingly, maddeningly – till he gave in.'

Alexander Walker

'Everything that girl does is sexy. A lot of people – the ones who haven't met Marilyn – will tell you it's all publicity. That's malarkey. They've tried to give a hundred other girls the same publicity build-up. It didn't take with them. This girl's really got it.'

Joseph Cotten

LA STORIA DI UNA DELLE DONNE PIU'
DEL NOSTRO TEMPO
DA
DEL SUO
Cine
marilyn
DI UN'EPOCA
20th CENTURY FOX

'Marilyn is a kind of ultimate, in her way... She is uniquely feminine. Everything she does is different, strange and exciting, from the way she talks to the way she uses that magnificent torso. She makes a man proud to be a man.'

Clark Gable

'What the hell is that girl's problem? Goddamn it, I like her but she's so damn unprofessional. I damn near went nuts up there in Reno waiting for her to show. Christ, she didn't show up till after lunch some days, and then she would blow take after take ... I know she's heavy into booze and pills. Huston told me there's something wrong with the marriage. Too bad. I like Arthur, but that marriage ain't long for this world. Christ, I'm glad this picture's finished. She damn near gave me a heart attack.'

Clark Gable

'By the end of the day, one thing was clear to me. I was going to fall most shatteringly in love with Marilyn, and what was going to happen? There was no question about it, it was unescapable, or so I thought; she was so adorable, so witty, such incredible fun and more physically attractive than anyone I could have imagined, apart from herself on the screen.'

Laurence Olivier

'She has a tremendous native feeling. She has more guts than a slaughter house. Being with her people want not to die. She's all woman, the most womanly woman in the world.'

Arthur Miller

'If she was simple it would have been easy to help her. She could have made it with a little luck.'

Arthur Miller

'It had to happen. I didn't know when or how, but it was inevitable.'

Arthur Miller

March 1959 · 35c

COSMOPOLITAN

SPECIAL ISSUE Manners and Morals

Swap-Mate Scandals He-Men and Honor in Business
Our Moral Revolt from 1920 to 1960 Is Divorce a Disease?
Lovelorn Sob Sisters Parents Review Sex Education

The New Marilyn
"SOME LIKE IT HOT"

istening Walls — Margaret Millar's Great New Mystery Novel

'It is Marilyn who is number one on all the GI polls of Hollywood favourites, and number one on exhibitors' polls of box office favourites. She is the number one cover girl of the year, and certainly number one in public interest wherever she goes.'

Louella Parsons

'The secret of her delicious sexuality, admired as much by women as by men, was that it raised rather than devalued the female currency. It was as sweet, natural and over-flowing as a burst peach.'

Donald Zec

'She knows the world, but this knowledge has not lowered her great and benevolent dignity, its darkness has not dimmed her goodness.'

Edith Sitwell

'Marilyn Monroe was the meteor of show business. There were many small, dim stars floating in the sky when the meteor streaked across the heavens. Its flash and fire blotted them into oblivion. Then suddenly the meteor was spent, plunged into darkness, and the small, dim stars could be seen floating in the sky again.'

Earl Wilson

'Dietrich made sex remote; Garbo made it mysterious; Crawford made it agonising; but Monroe makes it amusing. Whenever a man thinks of Marilyn Monroe, he smiles at his own thoughts.'

Milton Shulman

Carl Kain

'It used to be you'd call her at 9 a.m., she'd show up at noon. Now you call
in May, she shows up in October.'

Billy Wilder

'She could be just extraordinary – she could be sweet, she could be warm, she could be trying very hard. And then again she could be miserable, she could be unapproachable, she could be offensive, she could be rude, and worst of all, she just wouldn't show up, she wouldn't be around.'

Billy Wilder

PHILIP HAYS

'Beauty was part of her fascination. It contributed largely to it because it was unique. There was an article in a magazine once in which her masseuse was quoted as saying that Marilyn's flesh was different from other flesh. Well, there was something honeyed about her, something fetching. But as time went on, her beauty would have coarsened and that fragile, tremulous, lovely thing that we all witnessed would have been gone and then she would have lost her appeal because her appeal was largely physical.'

John Huston

'I suppose Monroe was just about the last of the female superstars to come out of the industry machine: she, fortunately, was spared the enormity of the self-destruct process that is ageing, though, God knows, one wishes she could have found some gentler way out.'

Alexander Walker

'It was almost as if she had been waiting for a button to be pushed, and when it was pushed a door opened and you saw a treasure of gold and jewels. It is unusual to find the underlying personality so close to the surface and so anxious to break out and therefore so quick to respond. This quickness is typical of great actors.'

Lee Strasberg

'We need her desperately. She's the only one of us who really knows how to act in front of a camera.'

Dame Sybil Thorndike

'She was a marvellous actress with a lively personality. Her life cannot have been very happy, but she always succeeded in appearing happy and serene.

Sophia Loren

'With silk-screening, you pick up a photograph, blow it up, transfer it in glue on to silk, and then roll ink across it so the ink goes through the silk but not through the glue. That way you get the same image, slightly different each time. It was all so simple – quick and chancy. I was thrilled by it. My first experiments with screens were heads of Troy Donahue and Warren Beatty, and then when Marilyn Monroe happened to die that month, I got the idea to make screens of her beautiful face – the first Marilyns.'

Andy Warhol

Marilyn by Andy Warhol 1964, © DACS 1984

'She built herself a career on overstating something, and she's made up her mind to understate. It's like herring à la mode. Put the chocolate ice cream on the herring and you spoil the ice cream, and the herring is no damn good either. They're trying to elevate her to a level where she can't exist. The lines the public really wants from her are not written in English.'

Billy Wilder

Clothilde Nadel

'Looking back, I guess I should have been excited, but I found her pretty dull. Marilyn spoke in a breathless way which denoted either passion or asthma. She wore dresses with the neckline so low she looked as though she had jumped into her dress and caught her foot on the shoulder straps … she used to carry around the books of Marcel Proust, with their titles facing out, although I never saw her read any of them. She was always holding up shooting because she was talking with someone on the phone. Judging from what's happened, though, I guess she had the right number.'

Jack Parr

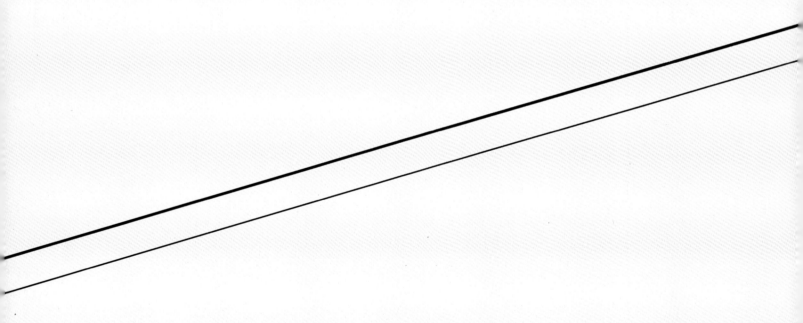

Clothilde Nadel

'She was a difficult woman, you know, we liked her and we said the nicest things about her and she deserved them; she was a very gallant person. But she was trouble and she brought that whole baggage of emotional difficulties of her childhood with her. She was very insecure and she had psychiatrists in attendance, if not every day then a number of times a week.'

Norman Rosten

'Marilyn Monroe was sensitive and very difficult. She tried hard, but you had to wait for her to come through, to start rolling, and then her kind of inhibition disappeared and after that she was phenomenal, one of the great comediennes.'

Billy Wilder

'In certain ways she was very shrewd. I once heard her talk in her ordinary voice, which was quite unattractive. So she invented this appealing baby voice. Also, you very seldom saw her with her mouth closed, because when it was closed she had a very determined chin, almost a different face. The face wasn't all that pretty, but it moved in a wonderful way, it was a wonderful movie face.'

George Cukor

'Directing her was like directing Lassie. You need fourteen takes to get each one of them right.'

Otto Preminger

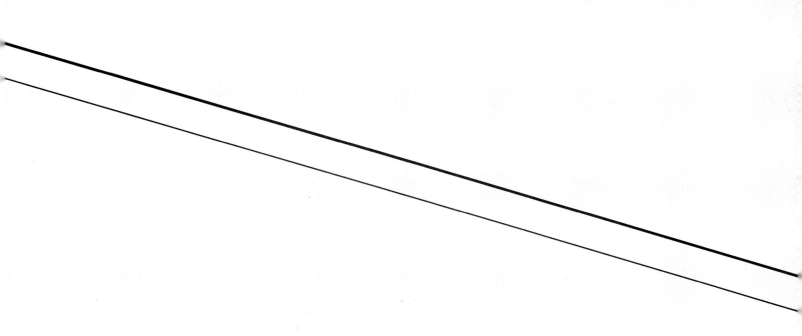

Oscar da Costa © Athena International

Dave Willardson/Windermere Press Inc

'She liked being a star. But she never put on airs or snobbish pretences with us. She was a marvellous, warm human being, wonderful to be around. She was the friendliest kind of person, always looking for a party, a good time. You know what she liked to do best? Laugh. Marilyn had a natural kind of humour. If she had fits of depression, they were behind closed doors. Sure, she was sometimes unhappy about her work. Every actor who is serious about his art gets that way occasionally. She had an intense desire to be better than she was.'

Peter Lawford

'She represents to man something we all want in our unfulfilled dreams. She's the girl you'd like to double cross your wife with. A man, he's got to be dead not to be excited by her. Yet what a terrible problem she has, conceive for yourself. How can one be a normal human being and do normal human acts, like for instance eating mashed potatoes, if one knows 15,000,000 men all over the world want to go to bed with one?'

Jean Negulesco

'In the beginning was the Flesh, and the Flesh became Word. Sex is the mysticism of materialism. We are to die in the spirit to be re-born in the flesh, rather than the other way round. Instead of the cult of the Virgin Mary we have the cult of the sex symbol – the busts, the thighs, the buttocks, of a Jean Harlow, a Marilyn Monroe, a Carroll Baker displayed in glossy photographs, on cinema and television screens, to be feasted upon by countless hungry eyes, the physical tensions thereby set up being subsequently relieved in auto-eroticism or in squirmings and couplings with an available partner. Eyes which launched, not a thousand ships, but a vast sea of seminal fluid; mistresses, not of kings and great ones, but of the Common Man, who clasps them to him and enjoys their wanton favours in his secret dreams.'

Malcolm Muggeridge

Pepe Gonzalez

'But in her movies – and perhaps this is why she is so potent a sex symbol – she shows no independence, no hardness, none of the amazing strength and drive of Norma Jean that got Marilyn *on* to the screen. The woolly-headed image of the Candle in the Wind is false.'

Polly Devlin

'Marilyn Monroe's unique charisma was the force that caused distant men to think that if only a well-intentioned, understanding person like me could have known her, she would have been all right. In death, it has caused women who before resented her frolicsome sexuality to join in the unspoken plea she leaves behind – the simple, noble wish to be taken seriously.'

Time Magazine

'Marilyn was not just another love goddess; she was one of the first love children, crossing over from America's conscience-ridden past into today's more open society. That she didn't quite make it to the other side had more to do with the harsh fundamentalism foisted upon her as Norma Jean than with her later intent as Marilyn.'

Fred Lawrence Guiles

'Miss Monroe has an extraordinary gift of being able to suggest one moment that she is the naughtiest little thing and the next that she's perfectly innocent. The audience leaves the theatre gently titillated into a state of excitement by not knowing which she is and thoroughly enjoying it.'

Laurence Olivier

'Marilyn didn't use expressions like "being made love to", she used a shorter, stronger word.'

Earl Wilson

Brad Marshall/TNT Designs Inc   Punz Wolfe

'Marilyn is a dreamy girl. She's the kind liable to show up with one red shoe and one black shoe… I'd find out when we'd take a break at eleven that she hadn't had any breakfast and forgot she was hungry until I reminded her. She once got her life so balled up that the studio hired a full-time secretary-maid for her. So Marilyn soon got the secretary as balled up as she was and she ended up waiting on the secretary instead of vice-versa.'

Jane Russell

'She would try to seduce the camera as if it were a human being ... she knew that the camera lens was not just a glass eye but a symbol for the eyes of millions of men; so the camera stimulated her strongly. Because she had a great talent for directing the entire impact of her personality at the lens she was a remarkably gifted and exciting model.'

Philippe Halsman

'She can make any move, any gesture, almost insufferably suggestive.'

Henry Hathaway
director

'She had a luminous quality – a combination of wistfulness, radiance, yearning – to set her apart and yet make everyone wish to be a part of it, to share in the child-like naiveté which was at once so shy and yet so vibrant.'

Lee Strasberg

Kenton R. Nelson

'People look the most kissable when they're not wearing make-up.
Marilyn's lips weren't kissable, but they were very photographable.'

Andy Warhol

'Kissing Marilyn Monroe was like kissing Hitler.'

Tony Curtis

Recycled Paper Products Inc

'Marilyn is completely feminine, without guile … with a million sides to her.'

Clark Gable

'She was not the usual movie idol. There was something democratic
about her. She was the type who would join in and and wash up the
supper dishes even if you didn't ask her. She was a good talker. There were
realms of science, politics and economics in which she wasn't at home,
but she spoke well on the national scene, the Hollywood scene, and on
people who are good to know and people who ain't. We agreed on a
number of things. She sometimes threw her arms around me, like people
do who like each other very much. Too bad I was 48 years older. I couldn't
play her leading man.'

Carl Sandburg

'She was the complete victim of ballyhoo and sensation. Popular opinion and all that goes to promote it is a horrible, unsteady conveyance for life, and she was exploited beyond anyone's means.'

Laurence Olivier

'I've hardly met a man who doesn't speak of her in wistful, protective, if-only terms. And women, too, love her now and think of her as a sister exploited by men, whom they could have helped with their new self-awareness and supportiveness.'

Polly Devlin

Michael Frith

'Imagine Marilyn alive today – very fat, boozing it up. I think she'd have
been a pitiful, dreadful mess and nobody would be able to remember
what they do remember, which is this incredible, off-beat, zany, wonderful
dizzy blonde. That's the way we should remember her and her death was
the best thing that could have happened to her.'

Joe Mankiewicz

'I knew it wasn't going to be a simple third act curtain for her. I just couldn't
visualise Monroe in a rocking chair or in the motion picture relief home or
married to somebody who was a pilot for United Airlines.'

Billy Wilder

Michael Frith

'This atrocious death will be a terrible lesson for those whose principal occupation consists in spying on and tormenting the film stars.'

Jean Cocteau

'If ever there was a victim of society, Marilyn Monroe was that victim – of a society that professes dedication to the relief of the suffering but kills the joyous. The evil of a cultural atmosphere is made by all those who share it. Anyone who has ever felt resentment against the good for being good, and has given voice to it, is the murderer of Marilyn Monroe.'

Ayn Rand
novelist

Marilyn pursued by Death: Rosalyn Drexler

THIS IS NOT THE MARILYN MONROE LEGEND. NOT EVEN THE WAY SHE TO

A GTO FILMS PRESENTATION
STARRING
MISTY ROWE AS NORMA JEAN BAKER
CO-STARRING TERRENCE LOCKE / PATCH Mackenzie /
SCREENPLAY BY LYNN SHUBERT / LARRY BUCHANAN /
MUSIC BY JOE BECK TITLE SONG WRITTEN BY JOHNNY C
AN AUSTAMERICAN PRODUCTION

THIS IS THE WAY IT WAS.

bye,

MAN

AN

X

NSON / MARTY ZAGON / ANDRE PHILIPPE
RY BUCHANAN
ORMED BY THE SUNDOWN COMPANY
E®AND TECHNICOLOR® GTO FILMS

'Monroe, at a studio other than Fox and paired with leading men other than the sexless freaks and mock lotharios she was always being saddled with, her image might have taken on the spiritual contours of a real woman (as Harlow's did) instead of constricting into a joke.'

Molly Haskell

'When I saw her up there [on screen] it was nearly incredible. The legend, which I thought a kind of joke in questionable taste, suddenly made sense. I could understand why all the fuss had been made, why the crowds went out of their minds whenever they caught a glimpse of her. It's a kind of magic. I never came to really like her, but I realised her worth as an actress, her value to any production.'

Angela Allen

'She had no handle on life, but by God, she had some other things that if you knew what they were you could sell the patent to Du Pont and they'd manufacture it. You would think that it's not difficult to make another Monroe; it should be easy – a blonde, small girl with a sweet face, my God, there should be thousands of them, they should come from all over the world.'

Billy Wilder

George Bevan

'I don't think she was an actress at all, not in any traditional sense. What she was … this presence, this luminosity, this flickering intelligence … could never surface on stage. It was so fragile and subtle, it could only be caught by the camera. But anyone who thinks this girl was simply another Harlow or Harlot or whatever is mad.'

Truman Capote

'It's Mae West, Theda Bara, and Bo Peep all rolled into one.'

Groucho Marx

Jean-Paul Vroom/© Victor Arnolds

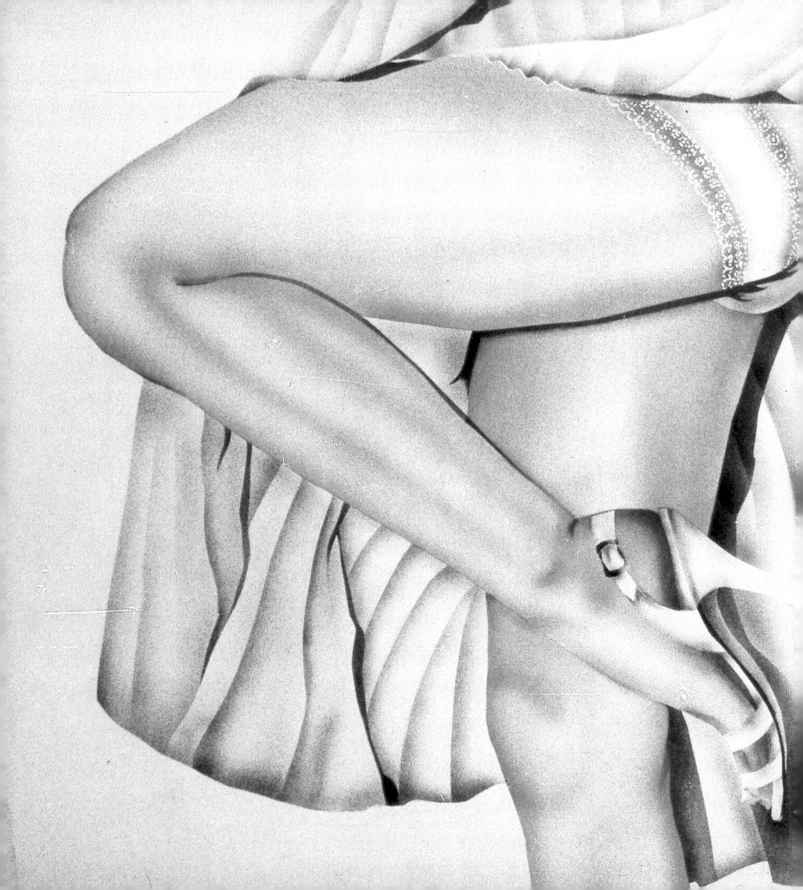